ALONG THE MAINE COAST

PHOTOGRAPHS BY KATHARINE KNOWLES, TEXT BY THEA WHEELWRIGHT

on the cover:
Stormy sea at Chamberlain

title page:
Bird's eye view of the rocks at New Harbor

opposite:
A fisherman paints his dory

Barre Publishers   Barre, Massachusetts
Copyright © Barre Publishers 1967
Library of Congress Catalog Card Number 67-14592
design: Shirley Errickson
composition: Arrow Composition, Inc.
printing: The Meriden Gravure Company

The Coast of Maine

The coast of Maine, as any seacoast, but more particularly Maine, is a study in contrasts: sun and shadow, hard winters, beguiling summers. Violent seas pound and gouge the coastal rocks, split the striated shale, up-ended eons ago by the receding glacier—and leave minute, brilliant, colored jewels of shell and stone in the sand.

The heron's lanky stillness and the chickadee's neat cheeriness are both Maine familiars. The hoarse, comfortable call of the red-winged blackbird is soon followed by the long-drawn, always distant, wistful song of the meadowlark. Of a Saturday evening, a good Maine meal will start with tasty but heavy beanpot beans—and end with a heavenly, fairy-light lemon meringue.

Stately mansions above sweeping, well-kept lawns guard Maine's heritage; snug saltwater farms hug her coast, and the sound of cowbells tinkling above the marshes is sweet on the air. Ramshackle outbuildings lean away from the prevailing wind—for every house must have its shed—and weather-beaten shacks nestle precariously upon spindly looking wharves, with stacks of lobster pots piled against them.

These are some of the elements that compose the environment of Maine coast towns. They lend magic to the very name of this northeastern state, whose coves and inlets and bays make up over 2,400 miles of coastline that is only 220 miles long when measured by crowflight.

Edna St. Vincent Millay grew up in Rockland, Maine. She knew and loved the feel of a seacoast town:

> *If I could hear the green piles groaning*
> *Under the windy, wooden piers,*
> *See once again the bobbing barrels,*
> *And the black sticks that fence the weirs,*
> *If I could see the weedy mussels*
> *Crusting the wrecked and rotting hulls,*
> *Hear once again the hungry crying*
> *Overhead of the wheeling gulls,*
> *Feel once again the shanty straining*
> *Under the turning of the tide,*
> *Fear once again the rising freshet,*
> *Dread the bell in the fog outside,—*
> *I should be happy—that was happy*
> *All day long on the coast of Maine.*
> *I have need to hold and handle*
> *Shells and anchors and ships again!*

From *Collected Poems,* Harper & Row, Copyright 1921, 1948, by Edna St. Vincent Millay.

opposite: Rockland Harbor

ITTERY

"A sup of New England's aire is better than a whole draught of Old England's ale," wrote the Reverend Mr. Higginson in his *1629 Journal of a Voyage to New England,* and especially is this true of Maine. Indeed, enthusiasts believe you can begin to feel the difference when you cross the bridge between Portsmouth, New Hampshire and Kittery, Maine. In summer, the air at once seems fresher and cooler. In winter, you can feel the dank stone-held cold of cities to the south melt from your heart in the generous warmth of the coastal sun.

Scarcely a town or city in Maine is without some tangible vestige of its first settlement, the earliest now well over three hundred and fifty years ago. Perhaps this is part of the state's special quality: her past and present are all of a piece.

Most New England settlements began as small clusters of houses hastily erected to face an inlet or the open sea, with the ominous unknown of thick forest behind them. At the first Indian alarm, families would crowd into the nearest houses that had been equipped as garrisons, or try to reach a communal, walled fort. The men would take their posts at the smaller windows above, from which they could fire at warriors trying to enter the first storey. There was no time to collect precious belongings.

The nightmare was that a child might be unaccounted for in the excitement.

During periods of active warfare, men were interrupted so often at their efforts to clear more land and grow more food that villages sometimes ran out of supplies and had to depend for days at a time on clams dug at great peril between raids.

The deep overhang of this hexagonal building is a characteristic feature left over from the original garrison, upon the site of which Fort McClary was erected in 1824 and named for the highest-ranking officer killed at Bunker Hill.

A far cry from those days was the mansion begun for Lady Pepperrell after the death of her famous husband Sir William Pepperrell, and finished some five years later, around 1765. But even during those years parts of Maine suffered Indian raids. For it was only in 1763 that the final treaty was signed which ended the insecurity and in many cases desolation caused both Indian and white man by the long series of French and Indian Wars.

Originally the cornices and columns and the doorway and window frames of the Lady Pepperrell House were a much darker shade than the rest of the building, which gave it a totally different appearance.

The Cutts House, York

*Y*ORK

Kittery, York, and Wells grew up together, formed the original, short-lived Province of Maine, defied the Indians together, built and rebuilt their towns over and over again. Most of the early properties were settled under grants from proprietors who had received large tracts of land direct from the King of England. In return for his piece of land, the settler might be required within a year to have built a good dwelling house, cleared several acres of land, brought it to good grass fit for mowing, and paid his share of the expense of building a meeting house and settling a Protestant minister. Obviously many a family would be forced to move on before they could establish a "good dwelling house" of any size. Sometimes it would be toward the more settled regions of Massachusetts; but often it would be farther up the rugged coast of Maine.

York was incorporated (1642) as Georgeana, the first and only royal city in America, and it was so called for ten years, at the end of which Massachusetts took over the Province of Maine "for its own protection," and Georgeana was given its present name.

By 1691 every town in Maine but Kittery, York, and Wells had been abandoned. The people were starving because the Indian raids had prevented them from growing enough corn. Most of their cattle had been killed by Indian snipers, or by themselves to feed the soldiers who had been supplied for their protection by Massachusetts, but were for the most part unruly as well as unfit to serve. The Historic Landmarks Association of York purchased Jefferd's Tavern, no longer an inn at the time, had it razed carefully, each timber marked and numbered, and had it all moved from its site in Wells township to York Village, where it was restored to its original form. Now it serves as a museum and perfect example of an early colonial tavern, with massive beams and huge fireplaces throughout. Somewhere along the line, one of the tavern-owners built an ingenious port-cullis-type door for extra protection of the small, oddly built bar.

During colonial times the keeper of a tavern was usually a respected, sober citizen of the town. For it was required by law that every village maintain an inn of some sort for travelers, and the General Court of Massachusetts was quite strict as to the rules by which these taverns were run. The kinds of food and drink served, and the prices for them, were prescribed by the Court, which during the 17th century forbade dancing and card playing.

The Cutts, House, shown at left, was originally built by Hugh Holman on a part of the York parish property sold to him in 1737. Robert Cutts, shipbuilder and ancestor of the man who married President Madison's young sister-in-law, took over the property.

It was on just such a snow-filled day—Candlemas Day in 1692, long before the Holman House was in existence—that the villagers of York were caught unaware. Indian attacks seldom took place in the cold of winter, but one of the most tragic massacres in American colonial history occurred that day. Around 150 Abenakis, part of a force sent down from Sillery, Canada, to forestall rumored English plans for snowshoe-company attacks upon the principal Indian villages, raided York. They killed wholesale—137 persons were killed or captured—they pillaged and burned, then forced their captives, among them women and children, to march to Canada no matter what their condition.

A curious coincidence links this massacre with a later one in Wells, the town where the fiery Reverend John Wheelwright, detested and banished by the early Massachusetts Puritans for his religious independence, had established a Unitarian church many years before. Two of the little girls captured in the York massacre, Mary and Esther Plaisted, were great-granddaughters of the Reverend John. They were placed in a convent in Montreal, where Mary eventually became a nun and finally the revered Mother Superior known as Marie des Anges. In the attack on Wells eleven years later, little seven-year-old Esther Wheelwright, also a great-granddaughter of the Unitarian minister, was captured and taken into an Abenaki chieftain's household. She grew up as an Indian child until, six years later, she was discovered by a Jesuit priest. After many negotiations with the reluctant chief, he was able to buy the little girl, who then became the ward of the Governor of New France, the Marquis de Vaudreuil, in Quebec. Esther was sent to the Ursuline Convent, and she, too, elected to become a nun, though much against her guardian's will. In time, Sister Esther Marie de L'Enfant Jésu became Mother Superior of the convent, where she remained until her death in 1780, a century after the death of her Catholic-hating ancestor. Her name is still an open sesame at the very beautiful French convent tucked behind its heavy walls in the heart of old Quebec.

Built opposite the Old Gaol on property leased from the parish for 999 years in 1766, the Wilcox House was at one time the first general store in York, run by Edward Emerson, a tailor. He opened a tavern there in connection with his store in 1780. Thirty-eight years later it was acquired by David Wilcox, and became famous under his management. The house, now privately owned, has been considerably altered, but is still noted for its twenty-five foot fireplace and the tremendous chimney arch in its cellar. Some of the most beautiful examples of intricate bricklaying are hidden in old cellars of Maine, forgotten though they still uphold the five-and seven-flued chimneys they were built to sustain.

The First Parish Congregational Church was built in 1747 to replace an earlier structure where the colorful Reverend Samuel Moody had begun his long pastorate. Among the many things told about him was his practice, upon spying a sleeping parishioner, to interrupt his interminable sermon and shout "Fire! Fire!" When the startled sleeper jumped up, calling out "Where?" the parson would roar back: "In hell, for sleeping sinners!" It took one hundred and forty years for the single stone dungeon, built as a "sufficient pryson" at York by a 1666 order of the Province Court, to become the combination stone and wooden building it now is. Until 1868 the county owned the Old Gaol. When it became town property the following year, it was put to many uses: as a lockup, a warehouse, a schoolhouse, and briefly, a private dwelling. It was repaired and restored by the Old York Historical Society and became a museum in 1900, at the suggestion of William Dean Howells, then editor of the *Atlantic Monthly*, and a summer resident of York.

York River is a tidal stream, and as such was the site of the first undershot mill in America, its wheels being turned by the changing tides' pressure against the bottom rather than by the flow of water over the top.

Sewall's Bridge, built in 1757, was the first of its kind constructed in this country. It rests on multiple piles bound together at the top with iron bands, but each cluster cut in a different length to fit the contour of the river's bottom. Major Samuel Sewall had to invent a pile driver for the job, and it was crude, but he was so successful that he was asked to superintend the building of a similar bridge across the St. Charles River in Cambridge.

The Sewall House, now the Elizabeth Perkins House, dating from 1730, can be seen across the river at the right in this photograph. Part of the house exists as originally built. A cigar-store Indian on the riverbank marks the supposed exit of an underground passage leading to the river bank as a means of escape from Indians. A trap door in the attic and a secret room in the cellar also suggest it may have been a wayside stopping place for runaway slaves.

Jefferd's Tavern and (opposite) the First Parish Congregational Church, York

York Beach in winter

*O*GUNQUIT

What is now Ogunquit Village officially became a part of the township of Wells in 1652. Most of its old houses have been turned to new use as summer tourist havens. Since 1903, when Charles Woodbury founded an art colony in the picturesque village, Ogunquit has been a center for the arts as well as a tourist's dream, with its rocky promontories punctuating its wide beaches. In the

1920's such artists as Hopper and Marin were painting here. George Bellows, Childe Hassam, Frederick Waugh, and many others were introduced to Maine shores at Ogunquit, and Mark Twain, William Dean Howells, and Richard Harding Davis also loved it in their time.

Is there anything, anywhere, lovelier than dune grasses blowing against sand and sea and skyline?

The beach at Ogunquit, two views

ELLS

Unlike those of Kittery and York, most Wells settlers were poor folk, who up to around 1700 lived in log houses, slept on mattresses made of cat-tail rushes, had no crockery or glassware—but they had their beautiful beaches stretching wide and long under ever-changing skies.

The gravestone—one of the few portrait stones extant in Maine—is that of Colonel John Wheelwright, son of the Unitarian minister of the same name.

opposite:
Winter seascape at Wells, taken from the King's Highway

KENNEBUNK REGION

One of the most gracious areas in Maine shares variations on the unique name "Kennebunk." Here Booth Tarkington summered and wrote his stories of innocent bygone teens; here also Kenneth Roberts lived and wrote the books that not only thrill generations of readers but are fine examples of historical accuracy.

The beautifully kept houses along these village streets reflect the owners' pride in their colonial heritage as well as the prosperity that began early with a thriving lumber and shipbuilding business.

The same keen eyes for balance that shaped the square-riggers built at Kennebunk Landing and towed down-river to Kennebunkport gave many of the village homes their graceful proportions.

Not the least of Kennebunk's beauties are the elms still standing from revolutionary days along its winding roads. The Lafayette Elm was so named on the occasion of the French General's being entertained in 1825 at the adjoining Storer Mansion—the home of General Joseph Storer, revolutionary soldier and personal friend of Lafayette. In later years, the considerably reconstructed house was the birthplace of Kenneth Roberts.

The famous Brick Store Museum was once a general store managed by William Lord, who was also active in shipbuilding and shipping interests. His heirs have not only developed the store as a museum, but have supplied it with a remarkable collection of early Kennebunk and Maine memorabilia.

A few oddities remain to season the serene beauty of the Kennebunks—some are gathered in the Trolley Car Museum. "The Wedding Cake House," on the road to Kennebunkport, boasts elaborate scroll-saw decorations added to the Georgian structure by a sea captain—so the local legend goes—to console his bride, who had been deprived of a wedding cake because of his emergency call to sea.

Church spires rise from every village in Maine and the Kennebunks are no exception. The South Congregational church in Kennebunkport is one of many beautiful and historical meeting houses in the area, though not the oldest.

The quiet world of Cape Porpoise is still centered around its fishing industry, as it has been since long before Pilgrim days. At one time it rivalled the township of Kennebunkport, of which it is now a part, in trading dried fish and lumber products for West Indies sugar, rum, and molasses.

The Storer Mansion and (opposite) Lafayette Elm

24

OLD ORCHARD

Sweeping along up the coast of York County, the public beaches of Maine soar through the wide stretches of Biddeford Pool to their climax at Old Orchard, one of the earliest and most famous bona fide seaside resorts in America. From here on, the rocky promontories no longer merely punctuate the miles of sandy beach, but begin to take over the coastline.

Casino and pier at Old Orchard Beach

𝒫ROUT'S NECK

Prout's Neck will be remembered not as the scene of Indian attacks now seldom recalled except as a thread or so in the tapestry of American colonial history, but as the place where Winslow Homer built his permanent studio, looking out upon the sea. He lived alone there, sometimes year round, while he created his powerfully realistic, luminous work. Writing on his 59th birthday in a letter to his brother Charles, Winslow Homer said:

"The life I have chosen gives me my full hours of enjoyment for the balance of my life. The sun will not rise, or set, without my notice, and thanks." One can believe it. Winslow Homer must have observed the sea with his whole being to be able to paint his tremendous canvases.

Winslow Homer's Studio and (opposite) Prout's Neck

PORTLAND AREA

As close to Maine's largest city as the shores of South Portland (the northern half of Cape Elizabeth until 1890), one finds the ubiquitous lobster shack.

Falmouth, as Portland was formerly called, lay helpless under bombardment from British vessels one entire October day in 1775, as punishment for the town's previous help to Boston. Forewarned, the town lost only one inhabitant, but over a hundred and thirty private homes, many of her public buildings, nearly every store and warehouse. All the wharves and all the vessels in the harbor, except two captured by the British, were destroyed. It is said that a Copley painting of the daughter of Alexander Ross of Falmouth was removed with others to an open field for safekeeping during the bombardment. Almost a hundred years later, Portland knew the ravages of fire again, when half the city was levelled. According to local historians, careless children played with fireworks that had been collected to celebrate the 4th of July, 1866, and at the same time the victorious cessation of the Civil War. Most of the city, therefore, is less than two hundred years old today.

Deep-water, ice-free, three and a half miles from open sea, the Port of Portland is one of the largest petroleum handlers on the east coast. Oil tanks dominate the scene, looking out from the Western "Promenade." Along Commercial Street, lobstermen and tugboats are tied up at the wharves that project unevenly from the shore. From one of these piers opposite the Custom House, a fleet of boats plies to and from the larger islands of Casco Bay, such as Great Chebeague, the Diamonds, Peaks Island, Cliff and Jewell Islands, and Bailey Island. Private boats in the greater Portland area of Casco Bay also know islands with intriguing names such as the Goslings, Bustins, Whaleboat, and Pound of Tea.

The City of Portland, with its Eastern and Western Promenades, overlooks the port at one end and farther reaches of Casco Bay at the other. Its shadowed Deering Oaks park, its cobbled waterfront street, its mansions and its brownstone houses, have the air still of an old New England sea coast town. Though Longfellow, around whose monument traffic swirls every day, is long since dead, one has the feeling that if he were to come back, despite the busy shoppers his former house now looks upon he would still feel at home. Even as Portland falls more and more into stride with modern trends, it carries its past along with it, especially in the old mansions that line so many of its streets.

A number of them have been the subject of famous paintings. Edward Hopper painted the Victoria House in 1927. At that time it was still called the Libby House, after its second owner. Originally built for Ruggles S. Morse of New Orleans as a summer house, it was really a palace, decorated in the Italian manner. It had been empty for thirteen years when it was purchased and restored in 1943, and given to the Victoria Society of Maine Women, who maintain it as a museum.

The house now belonging to the Portland Club was built from designs of Alex Parris for Richard Hunnewell in 1805. Nehemiah Crane purchased it, and nine years later sold it to Ether Shepley, who lived there till his death in 1877. The Portland Club acquired it in the 1920's from his son George.

The Sweat Mansion, now the Portland Society of Art building, has had a rather eventful history. It was built by Hugh McLellan, a descendant of one of the earliest pioneers of Gorham. No cellar was dug for it; instead, one was created above the ground. A wall of stone was erected, then sufficient loam was hauled and heaped up around the stones to create a cellar space. Hanson Brazier, a well-known craftsman of the time, was hired to finish the hall—and spent three months doing it. After the Embargo Act of 1807, which probably caused him hardship along with other Portland merchants, Mr. McLellan sold the house. General Joshua Wingate lived in it for a long time. His granddaughters sold it to Mr. Sweat, who lived there the rest of his life. At the death of his widow, the property was turned over to the Art Society.

Lobster shacks on the South Portland shore and freight yards along the waterfront, Fore River

A freighter steams toward Portland Harbor

33

A Portland dock, Custom House in the background

The Victoria Mansion, Danforth Street

The Longfellow Statue, sculptured in 1888 on commission from the city

opposite: The Sweat Mansion, now the Portland Museum of Art on High Street

below: A Portland doorway (Ether Shepley House), now the Portland Club on State Street

opposite:
A summer house
overlooks
Casco Bay
and below:
Deering Oaks Pond

Eastern Promenade

Panorama of Portland at dusk

FREEPORT

Toward the northern end of Cumberland County, sheltered by a series of jagged peninsulas from the open sea, yet with good access to Casco Bay, Freeport, now a quiet shoe manufacturers' town, was once one of the most active seaports in Maine. In 1820 it was also the scene of Maine's official birth as a state.

The town is divided into a number of villages. The heritage of some is centered on events that occurred during the Indian Wars. At Porter's Landing, industry was the keynote—a salt works, a blacksmith shop, shipbuilding yards all along the shore on down through South Freeport—and where is now a clogged-up estuary of Casco Bay, a good deep channel out to sea. At Mast Landing, masts for the King's Navy were delivered at the head of the Harraseeket River and shipped out, according to local legend, as early as the late 1500's. Now the river is a mere trickle through a salt marsh. The only industry it knows is that of cold busy hands at smelting time every April.

Freeport was the scene of the youth of one of America's foremost seafaring men and explorers. Commander Donald B. MacMillan came to live here with his sister. He worked his way through Freeport High School and through Bowdoin College, and began a teaching career that, in the classroom sense, ended when Peary invited him to be his assistant on his second and successful expedition to the North Pole. MacMillan's trips on the good ship "Bowdoin," with crews made up largely of students to whom their summer in the Far North became the high spot of their entire lives, were events of annual interest in Maine for many summers. His lectures on the Eskimos have been an inspiration to many thousands of listeners. Miss Knowles has followed the line north, taking pictures almost at random, to bring out the feeling of Maine. Its variations in architecture are fascinating to the photographer. Strange eccentricities such as the "Castle" at South Freeport, steeples, barns and garrisons and doorways; more modern Swiss-type chalets, primitive, uncompromisingly severe churches—even in the attempts at decoration—all have been subject of her roving eyes.

Casco Castle at Harraseeket Bay

Old Nazarene Church, Great Island

Fisherman's shack, Bailey Island, (above) an Orrs Island house

$\mathcal{O}$N THE KENNEBEC

At the wide, rolling mouth of the Kennebec River, along a broad spit of land created by the confluence of its waters and those of the Androscoggin into Casco Bay, is a fort built at the site of the first and shortlived attempt by the English to settle formally on the coast of Maine. Here two ships sent by Sir John Popham, who was determined to beat the French in colonizing the northeast coast of the New World, "anckored both together" with a total of 120 colonists aboard. They set about building a pinnace to use in trade along the coast, a storehouse for the supplies from the two ships, and fifty houses, a church, and a fort. An early, extremely severe winter set in, and all but 45 of the colonists elected to go back to England when the ships left. Of the remainder many died in the ensuing months, and in the spring the entire project was abandoned. But traces of the colony exist to this day. Only in the summer of 1965 was a bale seal (such as would be clipped to the ends of a bolt of cloth) found in digging the beach at Sabina Head that definitely established where the original fort and settlement were. Since it is a known fact that the particular seal found was manufactured in England between 1600 and 1622, this inscribed bit of lead also established the period of time during which the colony had to exist.

Phippsburg, of which the whole area of Popham Beach is now a part, was so named in honor of Sir William Phips, who became Governor of Massachusetts (then including the Province of Maine) in 1692. He was one of 26 children, 21 of whom were boys, and his life reads like a Horatio Alger story—from shepherd boy to adventurer, to knighthood, as the result of salvaging a Spanish galleon and recovering over a million dollars worth of gold for the King of England.

It was in Phippsburg that Benjamin Greenleaf painted his unique portraits, using oils and working in reverse on glass. He was the author also of a popular series of arithmetic textbooks used in the schools in the early 1800's.

A little farther up the Kennebec River, the City of Bath, always the scene of shipbuilding as well as lumbering and farming, is the only Maine port that builds steel ships for the U.S. Navy. But in its old houses along the river, in its superb marine museum, relics of the past still live to remind the beholder of a time when the Kennebec was, as Robert P. Tristram Coffin described it, "one of the best of all Maine cradles of manhood."

"The river stood first in eighteenth- and nineteenth-century history of lumbering," he wrote. "Logs for half the world came shooting down its rapids. Paul Bunyan took his American name and set his ax to his first tall trees here. Then, in the latter years of the nineteenth century the Kennebec ice became famous half the world over." Actually ice export had started with the successful shipment by an imaginative young Boston businessman, in 1805, of ice to the West Indies for the relief of yellow fever victims. By 1833 ice had been shipped to Calcutta, and it became a valuable and frequent cargo to far eastern ports as well as to South America. For many years New England farmers had a profitable crop that Nature gave them for the cutting.

Partly as a result of the ice trade, and of shipbuilding begun shortly before the Revolution, Bath was at one time Maine's busiest river port.

Along the Kennebec and (below) interior, Fort Popham

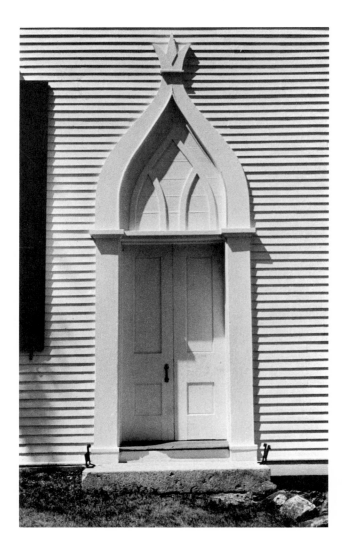

Details:
Steeple and church doorway, Phippsburg

opposite:
At sunset near the mouth of the Kennebec

"Spirit of the Sea" by William Zorach, 1962

Cupola, Bath City Hall

Interiors, Bath Marine Museum

WISCASSET

The beauty of Wiscasset goes back to the late 1700's and early 1800's, when most of her houses were built. It was the prosperous Georgian period when the West Indies trade was at its height. The town, because so little building has taken place since then, is one of the most perfect examples of an early American village that has not had to be contrived in any way. Since 1935 Open House Days—held annually at first, now every two or three years—are happy occasions when some twenty of its historical mansions are opened to the public.

It is hard to realize as one drives through this utterly serene town that it was the scene of many bloody battles between the Indian and the white man. The first settlement was wiped out at the beginning of King Philip's War and the area was deserted for nearly sixty years. Settlers who started to rebuild in 1729 had to erect a garrison fort first, for refuge against savage attacks that were still liable to occur. But by 1740 thirty brave families numbering some 150 persons had settled there.

Captain Samuel Doggett was responsible for the laying out of many Wiscasset streets. He had a proprietor's grant of 4,000 acres, and for each family he succeeded in settling on his land he received 25 acres more. To obtain one of Doggetts' 100-acre lots a settler had to agree to clear at least one acre each year fit for mowing or planting, and build a proper dwelling enclosed by a fence within seven years. If he fulfilled these terms the land was his for good.

Several legends are attached to the Carlton-Doggett house, recently bought by Mrs. David Greenlie from descendants of Samuel Doggett.

There is a story that the extremely wealthy Moses Carlton, one of the early owners of the house before it became the Doggett homestead, kept wheelbarrows of specie on hand for use by the bank—those being the days when a bank dealt more in cash than in credit.

This same Moses, according to a local legend, tempted fate outrageously. Standing at his wharf on the Sheepscot River, he suddenly drew a golden ring off his finger and threw it into the waters, exclaiming: "There is as much chance of my dying a poor man as there is of my ever finding that ring again." A few days later the ring was found in a magnificent fish being prepared for the wealthy man's table; and Moses Carlton did die a poor man, for an embargo tied up the 30 vessels on which his fortune depended.

Another story attached to this house concerns the impetuous bearer of news of the end of the War of 1812: Arriving at the town late at night, he saw lights only at the Carlton home, where a ball was in progress. In his excitement the man rode up the front stoop into the brightly lit hall and shouted the good news.

The quality of the hand-carved woodwork displayed in many Wiscasset houses, plus their architectural beauty, makes this town a mecca for the student of early New England culture. But it is also active in the contemporary art scene.

In 1955, Governor Edmund Muskie signed a bill conveying the Old Jail to the Lincoln County Cultural and Historical Association. The granite structure is being preserved for its architectural and historical significance. The attached brick jailer's house is now a museum devoted to ancient and modern Maine crafts. And housed in the former Wiscasset Academy building, the Maine Art Gallery, operated by a branch of the Association, offers the only juried exhibitions in the state. This means that any artist working in Maine has at least a chance of showing his work to the public.

The Governor Smith Mansion, originally built in 1792 for Silas Lee, a Harvard lawyer who became a judge and entertained lavishly, is another superb example of architectural detail, including its beautifully railed "widow's walk" or "captain's walk" on the roof. Lee lost the house in 1807, the year when the Embargo Act forced many a wealthy colonial esquire to sell out. Twenty-five years later it became the property of Governor Smith of Maine, with whose name the house is identified, and it has remained in the Smith family ever since.

The Nickels-Sortwell house was built by an unknown architect but one obviously influenced by Bulfinch, on the site of the first Wiscasset house of which there is any record. Captain William Nickels planned to entertain

Cupola, Carlton-Doggett House

lavishly; he had the old house pushed back and proceeded to put up his magnificent home in its place. The hand-carved woodwork inside and out is especially beautiful.

The Captain did not keep it for long and the house became an inn for many years. It was known as the Turner House, and as Belle Haven, and at one time—during Maine Prohibition days—it had a secret rum chamber.

In 1900 Alvin Sortwell and his wife purchased the building and restored it to its original beauty and use. It is now owned by The Society for the Preservation of New England Antiquities, who maintain visiting hours every day during the summer.

As one crosses the Sheepscot River on the low bridge past the derelict schooners that have leaned against the shore in a picturesque state of decline for many years one approaches the site of Fort Edgecomb. The most conspicuous landmark of the area, the blockhouse at Edgecomb is considered an excellent example of the military architecture of the War of 1812. It was built shortly before the war by the U.S. Government, under the direction of General Henry Dearborn, who was then Secretary of War.

A touch of the scroll-saw, Wiscasset

above left: Cupola, Maine Art Gallery
Gazebo at the jail

Antique shop, Wiscasset

Fort Edgecomb

$\mathcal{B}$OOTHBAY HARBOR REGION

The Boothbay Harbor region is a paradise for artists, whether with brush or camera. Small intricate coves vie with the open sea beyond, where windjammers spell happy vacations to hundreds of tourists every summer. Here is a place of provocative names: Powderhorn Island, the Ram Islands, Turnip, Crow, Hay, Tumbler Island, the Cuckolds, Paradise Point, Pig Cove, Molly's Head, Christmas Cove, the Ark—one could go on and on. The origin of some of these place names is easy to guess. In the early dangerous eternal quest for food, success merited a memorial. Others hint at long-lost tales of human emotions, relations, and events.

The prevailing southwest winds bring the Boothbay area sparkling days; the waters are brisk and inky blue; boats of every description, from old weatherbeaten lobster dories to such princely craft as the "Victory Chimes," the "Mary Day," and other lofty windjammers are at anchor along the docks, or careening across the bays and coves. Houses of every description from fishermen's shacks to the last word in "modern colonial" hug the slopes above. Gloomy thoughts of long-past massacre, hunger, war—of which this region had its ample share —seem out of place.

But behind the gay vacation facade there is a lot of good solid industry here. Fishing, of which around 90% is lobstering, is one of the main sources of income, and shipbuilding—mostly of pleasure craft nowadays—is so active that Boothbay is often called the boating capital of New England.

Shipyard workers, East Boothbay Harbor

opposite: Town Landing, Boothbay

Windjammer Days at Boothbay

East Boothbay Harbor Shipyard

The "Victory Chimes" at anchor in Boothbay Harbor

NEWCASTLE

The farther up the coast one goes in Maine, the more fascinating and varied are the antique shops. This one, on Route 1 in Newcastle, is one of the more elegant shops, but there are all kinds. A primitive display of rusty utensils may beckon the unwary from a house that seems utterly remote from any source of trade. A beautiful sign and exquisitely kept doorfront in a house that obviously was built in a period of opulence may frighten the amateur, but be filled with very fine objects of interest to the expert. Antique bargain hunting has become such a hobby for so many vacationers that most owners, even of the lowliest shops, know how to price their wares profitably. Still, traveling upon some apparently deserted road and coming upon the magic sign "Antiques," the hunter's hope always rises to the bait.

opposite: Antiques for sale at Newcastle

The Kavanaugh Mansion, Damariscotta Mills

THE DAMARISCOTTA AREA

One of the show places of Damariscotta Mills, the Kavanagh House was built by Nicholas Cobb, who put up a number of mansions in the area. As happened with a number of the early 19th-century mansions, the elegant hardware utensils for this house, the window-glass, etc., were probably imported from England. Many now prefer the crude but gracefully proportioned door latches and uneven-surfaced glass panes that were made in the colonies.

The Church of St. Patrick at Damariscotta Mills is the oldest functioning Catholic Church in New England. It was dedicated by a remarkable man, who later became the first Bishop in Boston. Father Jean de Cheverus had fled from France during its revolution, and he became a missionary to the American Indians. He lived a truly Spartan life, and was loved by men of all faiths.

One profitable facet of the lobster industry started at the Saltwater Farm at Damariscotta. People all over the USA, and beyond, can now eat fresh lobsters and clams shipped live in ice from the farm.

Of late years the crop of Maine lobsters has dwindled— but like the proverbial ill wind, this has brought some good with it. There is more profit for the serious, year-round lobsterman. He is getting a higher price for the scarcer commodity, and competition from the dilettante has decreased. The latter is more easily discouraged by empty traps than the seasoned worker, who is accustomed to putting in long, hard hours and pulling up as many as 500 traps in one day to find enough lobster gold.

Though men have been trapping lobsters for over 200 years on this coast, the industry is still young in terms of method and tools. There are those who feel that a differently designed trap would help; and all agree that a less strong-smelling bait would be a good thing all around. As it is, pleasure craft tend to shy away from wharves where barrels of stinking redfish are in evidence. Better and more modern pegging (plastic instead of wood), better packaging, better management as a whole —these are beginning to take over and may bring about changes in the business.

The Church of St. Patrick

Chapman-Hall House 1754 (restoration), Damariscotta

Saltwater Farm pier

Old firehouse,
now a gift shop
in Damariscotta

THE PEMAQUID AREA

The Pemaquid Patent—one of the oldest and most historical regions of Maine—originally encompassed a neck of land that included the present towns of Bristol, Walpole, Pemaquid, South Bristol, Christmas Cove, Pemaquid Point, New Harbor, and Medomak. Of these, the earliest settlement was in Ancient Pemaquid (1625), now Bristol.

above: Stone Fort William Henry, erected at ancient Pemaquid (1962) by Sir William Phips
opposite: Pemaquid Light
right: Sifting for treasures at Pemaquid

Harrington Meeting House (1772) Bristol

Christmas Cove

Back Cove, New Harbor, two views

When New England ships traveled to the Orient their captains brought back the objects that had caught their fancy, and put them alongside colonial furnishings; there was no clash between the two. It reminds me of the occasional interpolation of an Eastern-sounding phrase in Bach's and Haydn's music.

In a summer's morning fog, the Maine coastline suddenly assumes an Oriental look. A wispy band of mist will float just below pine treetops that loom black above it, or will obscure all but the gnarled branches of alders that have taken a precarious hold on the rocky shore. The water is still, a gunmetal gray, cut here and there by the silhouette of reflected hulls and masts of sailboats, quiet on their moorings. Sounds are intensified: the rhythmic beat of oarlocks as a dory fisherman goes the round of his lobster pots, the slow put-put of fishing boats, and quiet voices aboard, as they start out early to sea. These quiet noises in turn make the silence all the sharper. Then the dawn stripes the sky, there is the soft tearing sibilance of the changing tide along the beach, and the boats start a slow dance around their moorings as the rising sun casts a pale golden path across the water. The mists seem to cling briefly to the trees and weirs and docks before they dissolve into the light. Emerging stark and blue-black against the pearly sea behind him, I notice a heron, awkwardly graceful, still and patient, waiting for food to pounce upon; and I wonder how long has he been standing there? It almost seems as though it might have been forever.

Morning fog lifts at New Harbor

Children who grow up by the sea know an extra dimension, whether they are always aware of it or not. In the 1700's in Maine it was not unusual for a boy of fourteen to sow acres of corn, or drive an oxcart alone through hundreds of miles of coastal wilderness to join his family; or even spend a winter in a log cabin, alone with his dog, while his father went back for the rest of the family, so they could settle in the following spring! With all such a boy had to do making out for himself, there was probably no time to be bored, but what of loneliness and who knows how much fear? I wonder whether in his later teens such a boy took time out to emulate whatever the latest fad then—in beatnik terms—or did he simply go on, taking more and more responsibility? The chances are that by the time he was eighteen or nineteen, he was captain of his own square-rigger.

Boys of today who, like these two young fishermen, grow up in the quiet coastal towns of Maine at least have time to be children before they have to take on the fearful responsibilities of their generation. Perhaps they will have to tramp knee-deep in a fear-infested tropical wilderness, but the mathematical probability is that they will never have to depend upon their own physical powers for actual survival.

But in 1707 an exciting battle took place, at Winter Harbor, between 150 Indians in fifty canoes, and eight Englishmen and one boy in two shallops. They were holding off the Indians to allow the settlers on shore time to reach the safety of the garrison. It was a battle of wits and seamanship. In the end, though the Indians gained control of one of the shallops, the English, being better sailors, were able to rout them.

opposite: Watching the surf during a storm, Pemaquid area

Scarcely a village in Maine goes through a summer without an auction or two, and Miss Knowles has caught a familiar conglomeration of things and people in these delightful pictures. One can hear the auctioneer's rapid patter: "I have this antique pair of frames—pictures in 'em too. How much am I offered? Fifty. Who'll make it seventy-five? Seventy-five, who'll make it a dollar? A dollar. Who'll make it a dollar and a quarter? A dollar and a quarter, anybody? A dollar and a quarter, who'll make it a dollar and a half? Any bids? Sold: to the lady in the second row, for one dollar and a quarter."

Men, women, children mill around, fingering this or that, ready to laugh at the auctioneer's quips, hoping for a bargain, often, spurred by their neighbors' bids, paying a lot for something they really didn't want in the first place.

Village auction at Round Pond

The Village of Round Pond in spring

Muscongus Bay from the Audubon Camp at Medomak (looking toward Hog Island)

Interior and exterior, Old German Church, Waldoboro

WALDOBORO

Many different cultures are represented in the State of Maine. Permanent settlement of the Waldoboro area was made by Germans seeking religious freedom. They thought they were to find a church, a town house, and buildings ready for them to live in. Instead, a few shacks stood on the shore, with a frightening wilderness in the background, and the trees already taking on the metallic look of coming winter. Many suffered privation during the first year; one group was able to split off and go south to the Carolinas. Some went west. The remainder managed somehow to survive, and in the end they had a prosperous community. At the height of the shipbuilding era, Waldoboro's brigs, schooners, barkentines, and clipper ships—28 vessels launched in 1848 alone, for example—were sailing all over the world.

During its earlier history, Old Broad Bay, as Waldoboro was first called, lacked the religious leadership the citizens craved. The Reformed Lutheran Church was finally built in 1772 by a group of settlers who decided to take matters into their own hands. It was moved to its present site in 1794, and that year, finally, the Lutheran parish had a real shepherd. Then, as more and more Puritans settled in the area and members of the parish spoke less and less German at the turn of the century, Lutheranism began to decline. Now the old church is closed most of the time.

FRIENDSHIP

The Friendship Sloop, some thirty years ago, was thought to be dying out, but the designs for this beautiful lobster-fishing sailboat have been revived. The town associated with these boats each summer invites Friendship sloop owners from all over the country to gather for a three-day regatta, "The Homecoming Races," during which the host town lives up to its name with warm hospitality. The sloop itself, with its gaff rig, sharp clipper bow, and overhanging stern with elliptical transom, was designed for lobstering by its first builders, who were fishermen. Each builder added some new note to the basic design. Wilbur Morse, who built his first one for himself at the age of twenty-one, and sold it at the end of the lobstering season, was responsible for this particular type of sloop being associated with the town of Friendship. By the time he was twenty-nine he had a thriving shipbuilding business there, and soon other builders joined him.

When these beautiful wooden ships were superseded by plastic and metal boats, and quarrying, Friendship's other main industry, died out, the town simply reverted to its original role as a lobstering center. Now, out of a total population of around 800 persons, over a 100 men are licensed to haul lobsters.

Lobster traps, Friendship

THOMASTON

Driving through the wide, elm-shaded main street of Thomaston (home of the forbidding state prison), one makes a sharp right turn up a steep incline, past Montpelier, a superb reconstruction of the mansion built in 1793-94 by General Henry Knox.

A bookseller by trade, he became commander of the artillery during the Revolution. He and his younger brother were responsible for the transportation of valuable siege guns, captured at Ticonderoga, to George Washington at Boston. It seemed an utterly impossible task, during the bitterest winter season. But the brothers arranged for relays of oxen, and the deed was accomplished, with great effect upon the course of the Revolution. General Knox and his wife became close personal friends of George and Martha Washington, during the years 1785 to 1794, when Knox was Secretary of War.

The general and his wife entertained lavishly at Montpelier. As many as a hundred beds would be made and an ox and twenty sheep slaughtered for food in one week. After Knox retired from the army, he developed several business enterprises, brickmaking, lime, sawmills, logging operations, a large mercantile business—and it is not surprising that many of the houses in Thomaston have the look of a mansion about them, for his pursuits brought prosperity to the town.

Following the incline past the Knox mansion one drives down a winding road through the St. Georges River region, past Tenants Harbor, Martinsville—where Sarah Orne Jewett wrote her *Country of the Pointed Firs*—finally out to Port Clyde, from which a daily ferry goes to Monhegan Island.

One of the most attractive harbors in Maine, Port Clyde is the home of the impressionist, William Thon; for some years Andrew Wyeth, whose unique work brings out the poetry of ordinary objects, also had a studio here. Sarah Orne Jewett used to observe the older lobstermen at work in Port Clyde, and her character-sketches of them are classic:

. . . There were four of these large old men at the Landing, who were the survivors of an earlier and more vigorous generation. There was an alliance and understanding between them, so close that it was apparently speechless. They gave much time to watching one another's boats go out or come in; they lent a ready hand at tending one another's lobster traps in rough weather; they helped to clean the fish, or to sliver porgies for the trawls, as if they were in close partnership; and when a boat came in from deep-sea fishing they were never far out of the way, and hastened to help carry it ashore, two by two, splashing alongside, or holding its head steady, as if it were a willful sea colt. . . . My friend, Captain Bowden, who was the nephew of the eldest of this group, regarded them with deference; but he did not belong to their secret companionship, though he was neither young nor talkative. "They've gone together ever since they were boys, they know most everything about the sea amon'st them," he told me once. "They was always just as you see 'em now since the memory of man."

Montpelier (opposite) and Thomaston's Main Street

Two views of Port Clyde

MONHEGAN

The island of Monhegan was reported by Captain John Josselyn to be one of a number of communities between the Kennebec River and Nova Scotia that had a promising number of dwellings. His description of the people

of Maine at that time is of interest. Dividing them into three categories, magistrates, planters and fishers, he went on to say that some were Royalists like himself, but the rest were a perverse lot who took tobacco, slept at noon, sat down to as many as four meals a day. He claimed they worked only when it was necessary for their livelihood.

That still seems to be a characteristic of many Maine people! There are many workmen in this state who simply want to make a good living, with an accent on the *good*. They are not interested in trying to make a fortune. They take time out when the hunting season comes; they work hard, but they also know the value of leisure and the pleasure their beautiful land can offer them. Most likely the men who "slept at noon" to Josselyn's scorn had earned that sleep. The average lobsterman, starting to work as he does before dawn, has already done a day's work by noon; as for the four meals, a man who is up that early and works that hard can use more food than the ordinary sedentary mortal.

But to get back to Monhegan: it was a landmark for many of the early explorers. In 1605 Captain Waymouth anchored off the island and named it St. George. In 1614, Captain John Smith, sailing in search of whales and gold and copper mines, found the island, too. And instead of gold, he saw a harbor teeming with fish. It was Smith's report that encouraged Ferdinando Gorges, the man most responsible for the settlement of Maine, to continue promoting the New World.

Monhegan is one of the most beautiful islands on the Atlantic Coast and has long been the home and inspiration of many artists. Robert Henri started his school there in the early 1900's and was followed by many brilliant young men who carried on his tradition, among them, Rockwell Kent, who settled on the island when he was twenty-three and did some of his finest paintings there. George Bellows was another; many of John Marin's paintings vibrate with Monhegan light and color and movement. The island is still a mecca for artists, and there is no mistaking its impact upon their work.

opposite: Sunset from harbor shore, Monhegan

ROCKLAND

A busy port, Rockland, her docks always alive with the bustle of wings and hungry shrieks of gulls that have followed the trawlers in. Loud and long are their quarrels as they swoop down and fight for the "gurry" thrown overboard.

The Rockland Ferry daily plies back and forth to Vinalhaven and other islands across the bay. The city has consistently engaged in fishing, shipbuilding, and limestone quarrying—the latter industry determining its name some years after it was separated from Thomaston, of which it was originally the eastern section.

One of the most satisfying art museums in the east, many people believe, is the Farnsworth Art Gallery, where not only is the lighting particularly excellent, but the exhibits are never crowded on the walls.

The average visitor to the gallery is probably unaware that its presence and dedication to the promotion of beauty and art result from a lifelong, bitter, neurotic unhappiness. The Farnsworth homestead had been the scene of a rather familiar story: the handsome, fun-loving father, impatient with his plain-faced older daughter, had affection only for the beautiful younger girl. Lucy Farnsworth, desperately lonely, longing to be part of her father's life, was finally left with the house and a quarter of a million dollars inheritance. She shut herself in the house and lived like a miser until her death, alone and undiscovered for several days. She hated her own face so much that she destroyed it in all the family portraits. Her estate had grown to over a million dollars and her will decreed that the money should be used to create a museum and restore the Farnsworth home to its original beauty; and this has now been done.

The big trawlers that go to far-off fishing banks are gone for several days at a time. They have to have plenty of ice aboard to keep their catch fresh. The fish is usually processed to some extent on the way back to the joy of the ever-present convoy of gulls.

Fishing weirs, still pronounced "wares" here, in good Elizabethan style, have been in use since Indian times. They are simply traps for the fish, who, once they have entered the enclosure made by the poles, mill around waiting to be hauled in by fishermen with long-handled dipnets. Modern methods of fishing have superseded the weirs for the most part, but they are still in use and lend a note of archaic beauty to a seascape here and there.

Part of Rockland's success as a port is the protection given its harbor from the east by the rocky neck of land from which Owl's Head Light is a welcome sight to ships at sea.

opposite: Trawlers, Rockland dock

Workmen on the waterfront at Rockland

The mackerel boats, Rockland

97

CAMDEN

Perhaps spurred by the natural beauties of its harbors and the land rising above the sea, not only at Camden proper but at what is now Rockport, citizens of this area seem to take particular pride in beautifying the town. The flowered lamp-posts, well-kept, gracious houses, and charming shops bear witness to it.

One of the many gala affairs, including gymkanas and sulky races that take place during Maine summers and at many of the autumn fairs, is the Camden Horse Show. Morgans, Arabians, quarter horses (used to work with cattle), and several other breeds are raised all over the state. With so many wonderful wood trails still free of macadam, there is more and more enjoyment here in simple horseback riding.

A Camden lamp post

opposite: Camden Harbor, one of the most enchanting in Maine, and the berth of windjammers

View of Camden Harbor from Mt. Battie

On Mt. Battie, a memorial to veterans of World War I

ℬELFAST

Some of the most beautiful mansions in Maine—not to mention its touches of the scroll-saw era—are in the City of Belfast, about halfway up the coast, at the mouth of the great Penobscot River, the scene of naval battles during the War of 1812. For a time the cities and towns along the Penobscot as far up as Bangor were virtually in possession of the British.

The broad deep waters of the Penobscot could not only float millions of logs from sawmills upriver, but were navigable to large freighters. For some years Bangor, many miles above Belfast, was the busiest lumber export center in the world. During the 1860's as many as 250 vessels—schooners, square-riggers, "down-easters"—have been in the port at one time. Sometimes two tugs would tow as many as 27 lumber schooners, lashed in groups of three abreast, downriver to the open sea.

opposite: The Hydton House, Belfast, said to have been built from plans drawn by Sir Christopher Wren

below: A Belfast home; every town in Maine has a touch of the scroll-saw

*B*UCKSPORT

This town played an important role in the busy lumber transport scene.

Protected by Fort Pownal (1759), the site of the present Fort Knox, more and more settlers moved into the Bucksport area, until by 1776 there were some twenty-seven families and an "army" of fourteen soldiers. These marched to Castine to join the unsuccessful Penobscot Expedition against the British. In reprisal, the ship of war "Nautilus," after the American retreat from the siege of Castine, anchored in Bucksport Harbor and landed a crew of men who set fire to the town while the inhabitants fled through the woods. But the area was re-settled in 1784, and by 1801, Bucksport was one of the largest towns in the eastern section of Maine.

opposite:
The Bucksport Bridge across the Penobscot River

below: An inland view of the Penobscot

The annual Retired Skipper's race, Castine

CASTINE

From here on to Eastport, its farthest reach, the coast of Maine is so jagged that it is bewildering to try to trace it on a map of the state. Castine, at the tip of the first large peninsula below Bucksport, was early settled and incorporated and has been the scene of some of Maine's most colorful historical events. Named for the Frenchman who had so much to do with its development, it exchanged hands several times before Maine became one of the United States in 1820. The early trading post run by Pilgrims at the site of Castine was raided by French buccaneers in 1632, and again in 1635, at which time the Pilgrims gave it up. From 1640 to 1651 Castine was often the scene of conflict between D'Aulney, a Catholic explorer interested in gathering lands for France, and La Tour, a Huguenot, interested in the same thing, under a different persuasion. In 1656 Biguyduce, as it was then called, was taken over by the British, during the conquest of Acadia. In 1668 the Treaty of Breda turned Acadia over to the French again, and it was at this time that Baron Castine first established his trading post there and made friends with the Indians of the Etchemin tribe. He married the daughter of Chief Madockawanda and was adopted into the tribe. Castine was a friend of the British also, until his post was attacked and robbed by a roving expedition led by a British noble. From then on Castine and Madockawanda sided with the French in the wars that followed.

In 1703 the Baron had gone back to France and his son had succeeded him at the fort. A band of Englishmen, pretending friendship, robbed and plundered the young man's home. Though the colonial authorities promised to make restitution and punish the British, the Indians remained angry at the insult to a blood brother's family. This was one of the events, in fact, that fired the Indian attack in August 1703 upon Wells and other towns. A peace treaty signed at Utrecht between the English and the French in 1713 brought some respite to the colonists, but not for long. By 1721 the Indians from Penobscot and young Castine met with Norridgewock Indians and Father Rasle, the recalcitrant Jesuit who had become a leader of Indian resistance, and they declared war on the colonists. It was the beginning of a series of brutal and bloody skirmishes that went on for five years before a treaty was signed between Governor Dummer of Massachusetts and the Penobscot sachem and 25 sagamores, representing all the eastern Indians.

During the Revolution, the British general Francis Mc-Lane took over Bagaduce, as it was then called, with a force of 900 men, and proceeded to put up fortifications. The authorities in Boston were so alarmed at the news that they sent sea and land forces, which set out from Boothbay Harbor to recapture Bagaduce. Unfortunately, though the land forces were successful, the commander of the fleet was overcautious, and in the end not only were both routed by the British, who sent reinforcements from Halifax, but the entire coast and the coastal islands were captured. The British garrison remained at Castine for four years, until the Treaty of 1783.

During the War of 1812, though the commander of the fort at Castine blew up the redoubts and spiked all the guns before surrendering to the more numerous invaders, their capture of Castine gave them control of the Penobscot.

Now Castine is the berth of Maine's Maritime Academy and the site of some of the most beautiful houses in the state, from the simple colonial, low-ceilinged small buildings on the shore to stately mansions with typical fan doorways along its quiet elm-lined streets. And as in all the seacoast towns, the individual and independent sea captain builder of Maine has left his mark, sometimes showing clearly the influence of the Far East.

In her evocative *The Little Locksmith*, Katharine Hathaway has caught the very special quality and effect Castine has upon newcomers: ". . . I began to be dimly aware of the genius loci which inhabits Castine . . . a strong unseen presence," she writes, "which if we were ancient Greeks would surely be given the name of a god and be honored by us with an altar in the Witherle Woods; because it is an influence which takes quite simple, everyday human beings out of themselves and astonishes them during that short, exciting season, with the sudden acquisition of many charming personal qualities they never had before."

opposite:
The training ship "State of Maine"
can be seen in the background, anchored
at the Marine Academy dock, Castine

Sea Captain's House, Castine

DEER ISLE

Some forty minutes from Castine and across a bridge from Sedgwick, lies Deer Isle, which was also the scene of many battles during the Revolutionary War and the War of 1812. For many men in Stonington, on the tip of Deer Isle, the major industry is at the quarries on nearby Crotch Island. For eight months, during 1965-66, from the icy winter through blistering summer heat, 100 men were rowed over to the island each day to blast out, cut down, and polish 1,500 pink and gray granite stones, earmarked for a very special purpose. These stones, some weighing as much as 6,500 pounds apiece, are dovetailed into place at the John F. Kennedy gravesite at Arlington, Virginia. Seventeen of them have been inscribed with passages from President Kennedy's Inaugural Address, in lettering designed by John Benson, one of America's finest calligraphers.

Two views of Stonington, on the tip of Deer Isle

Waterfront at Stonington on Deer Isle

The Black Mansion, Ellsworth, where many George Washington memorabilia are preserved

BAR HARBOR

Noted for its mangnificent scenery, and for over 100 years called Eden, Bar Harbor during the gay nineties was the summer home for some of the wealthiest socialite American families, but a disastrous fire in 1947 wiped out most of the community, and it hasn't been the same since. On the outer regions of Mt. Desert Island, of which Bar Harbor is part, is the Acadia National Park, site of Mt. Cadillac, the highest peak in the nation located so near the sea.

opposite: Seen from Mt. Cadillac on Mt. Desert Island

Rock cliffs along the Shore Drive, Bar Harbor

Beach at Bar Harbor, along the Shore Drive

Seen from Mt. Desert Island

$\mathscr{F}$RENCHMAN'S BAY AREA

The fishing villages and towns along Frenchman's Bay are graced with scenes of magic beauty. All have their steeples rising white above the houses, with as varied architectural features as the characters of the people who worship in the meeting houses and churches from which they soar. The harbors are deep and safe, and replete with lobster shacks and Nova Scotia built lobster boats, with their high prows and long sloping sweep to the stern.

opposite:
Morning fog over Frenchman's Bay at Winter Harbor

and below: Mt. Desert Island seen from Sullivan (Frenchman's Bay)

below: Schoodic Point

Church steeple, Prospect Harbor, Frenchman's Bay

Meeting House steeple, Prospect Harbor

Corea Harbor, Frenchman's Bay

Machias

One of the most exciting episodes of American revolutionary history took place at Machias (now divided into three towns), but its settlement began over a century before that. In fact, in 1527 Captain John Rutt, an Englishman, made a map of the island waters about it and placed a cross on what is still named Cross Island. Machias was the ideal site for a fur trading post, for it was the terminus of canoe routes from the Penobscot Valley on the west and the St. Croix on the east. Hundreds of Indian tribes gathered each autumn at the mouth of the Machias River, as evidenced by the enormous shellheaps they left behind.

The first permanent settlement was by people who had been driven to seek new sources of fodder and lumber by a drought and series of fires in southwestern Maine. Some two dozen families settled there in 1763 and during the year sawed nearly 1,600,000 feet of lumber! They were making their own bricks before 1773, as well as their own salt on the island still called Salt Island.

The "Margaretta" was the first British vessel captured by the Americans, and the incident, which took place soon after the Battle of Lexington, reads like fiction, even to the desperately needed powder and lead for this first battle being carried twenty miles through the forest, from Jonesboro to Machias, by seventeen-year-old Hannah Watts, and her younger sister.

It all began when Captain Ichabod Jones of Boston obtained permission to carry a shipload of provisions to Machias, where some of his relatives were, on condition that he return with a cargo of lumber for the British troops. To make sure he fulfilled his part of the bargain, the "Margaretta" was sent along as convoy. She was a small vessel, but mounted several cannon. This was too much for Machias patriots, who loathed the idea of their town supplying anything for the British.

A few of them met in the tavern of Job Burnham and decided on a liberty pole in the town square as a protest.

Moore, the British captain, was incensed at sight of it and ordered the pole to be taken down, or he would fire on the town. Machias townspeople were defiant and voted against the move. Moore was ready to fire, but Jones persuaded him to wait while the villagers held one more meeting. Meanwhile, a band of the patriots decided to take matters in their own hands. They plotted amongst themselves to capture the British officers while they were at church. The plot was discovered and the Redcoats escaped on board the "Margaretta," and sailed her downriver, nearer the open sea.

Aroused by their failure, a group of about sixty men gave chase, armed with everything they could lay hands on from guns to pitchforks. Forty men were aboard Jones's sloop and twenty aboard a small schooner. The latter grounded, but Jones's ship caught up with the British. At the end of a bitter fight the warship had to give up. News of the successful capture of the British vessel traveled quickly down the coast and heartened the colonists everywhere.

A garrison was set up at Machias, and by 1777 it had become a full military station, Fort O'Brien. Men in Machias had been helpful to and traded fairly with the Indians. This was fortunate, for when the British attacked the Fort, after they took Castine, some fifty Indians assisted the small force available, and their method of warfare, their war whoops and guerilla tactics, terrified the British, who fled in retreat.

The town was not so fortunate in 1814 when after taking over the Penobscot area the British arrived in force to attack the fort. Unable to defend themselves, the hundred men at the garrison destroyed the cannons, set the place on fire, and abandoned it completely.

The Burnham Tavern (1770) and interior, Machias

below: The town of Machias from across the river

CUTLER

Besides having one of the best and deepest harbors on the Atlantic Coast, and a lookout point from which on clear days the Bay of Fundy can be seen, Cutler is the site of the most powerful radio station in the world. Twenty-six towers enable the station to send radio signals to atomic-powered submarines, and to detect missile launchings and nuclear explosions all over the world.

For many years blueberries have been an increasing product of Maine, along the coast as well as in the interior. Aside from its economic aspects, there is a very special quality to the New England blueberry harvest season, which arrives often when a crisp hint of fall is in the early morning air but the earth still holds the warmth of summer, and the berries have a dewy frosted look in the warm midday sun.

The sleepy, spired town of Lubec and the island city of Eastport, of which Lubec was once the mainland, are often thought of as the "Land's End" of the United States.

As I write this brief accompaniment to the photo study Miss Knowles has made of Maine's coast, it is early morning in September. A golden dawn seems to have thrown its yellow light into the early bright blue of a glorious day, and the trees are a more brilliant lush green than ever as the light streams through them. It is hard to believe that a week from now those same leaves will have a metallic sheen as they begin to take on autumn fire.

In a couple of months the wild geese that heralded the delicate, lacy foliage of a Maine spring, in triangles across the March sky, will honk their salute to another robust winter, on their way back south.

opposite: Harbor shore at sunset, Cutler

Blueberry pickers in Washington County

Along the shore of Passamaquoddy Bay

Two examples of Eastport architecture

Quoddy Head Light,
easternmost point of the U.S.A.

The Canadian Islands,
from Eastport